THE TAO OF SAILING

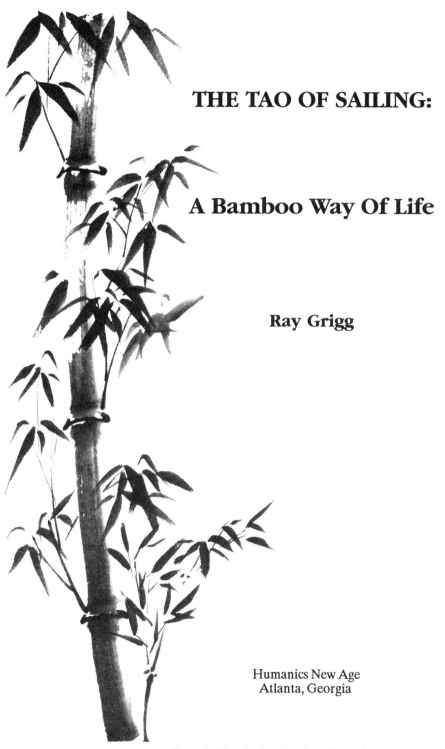

THE TAO OF SAILING:

A Bamboo Way Of Life

Ray Grigg

Humanics New Age
Atlanta, Georgia

Humanics New Age is an imprint of Humanics Limited

Humanics New Age
P.O. Box 7447
Atlanta, Georgia 30309

Humanics New Age is an imprint of Humanics Limited

PRINTED IN THE UNITED STATES OF AMERICA

Library of Congress Cataloging in Publication Data

Grigg, Ray, 1938-
  The Tao of sailing: A Bamboo Way of Life
/ by Ray Grigg.
    p. 176
  ISBN 0-89334-138-X
  1.Lao-tzu. Tao te ching. 2. Sailing. 3. New Age movement.
I. Title.
BL 1900.L36G75 1990
299'.51482--dc20   90-30317
                                            CIP

To Frank Braithwaite

And to the
Zair
Zita
Matuku Moana
Fairwinds
Fomalhaut
Atalanta
Avenger
Babalatchi

There is a way of being that cannot
be known until we release to wind and
waves on the sea of unknowing.

With mind poised just so...empty
and full of sky...a way becomes clear.

The Titles of the Chapters

Ship

Sea

Sailor

INTRODUCTION

Sailing is sagely. When we sail we make our own way in the world while recognizing and honouring the greater way of things. We are like the Taoist sage who balances volition and compliance by using what is given rather than taking what is not given.

The balance of the whole requires that we individually come to an understanding with the collective way of things, what the ancient Chinese called the Tao. But how do we find this wise and special way of being that fulfills the needs of the particular and the general? Within the bounds of birth and death, how are we to live fully and harmoniously and graciously? How are we to be with this world like a sailor is with wind and sea?

When we sail we enact the wisdom that is the Tao's way. We move in accord with the energy of wind and sea. With waves we rise and fall just-so. With wind we go or stay just-so. We move with the body of sea and the breath of air, changing in abidance with a breathing that is larger than ourselves.

Our own thinking and our own doing is the wind and sea of ourselves. When we attune ourselves to the larger breathing, we experience a deep harmony. In this deep harmony we sense the ways and rhythms of the larger breathing so we may enter it and join in balance with our larger body that Taoists call the Great Mother.

This book is about how we, as ordinary people, might live more beautifully with ourselves and with the wider world merely by being attentive and receptive, patient and responsive, to what is around us and within us. For sailors specifically, THE TAO OF SAILING is about the spirit of sailing. For readers generally, it is a metaphor for a way of living.

Bamboo and sailing - each is a metaphor for grace, beauty, resilience, balance, resourcefulness. Each has a mystique that is poetic, aesthetic, spiritual. Bamboo is to the East what sailing is to the West - each embodies the wisdom of a special way of being.

This special way of being is accessible to everyone. Although sailors will benefit from their knowledge and experience of sailing, each person who reads this book is a sailor upon the sea of life.

A Taoist way of life is both a bamboo and a sailing way of life. When we live this way of life, things seem to happen with an ease that is natural and timely - like bamboo growing from soil, like a sailboat moving upon sea. Even in the winds of adversity an inner balance steadies the heeling ship, a firmness of root holds beneath the bending bamboo.

Bamboo, as one of the most traditional of Chinese images, broadens and deepens the connection between the Western activity of sailing and the Eastern philosophy of Taoism, affirming that the sailor's practice is also the Taoist's. Furthermore, bamboo is a page by page reminder that the words that accompany the illustrations should move beyond the stiffness and confinement of the literal toward the richness and expansiveness of the metaphorical.

Because sailing is intended as a metaphor, illustrating this book in a strictly representational manner simply would not do - it would merely narrow the evocative range of the words. Although bamboo is used to create an Oriental atmosphere that is appropriately Taoist, it is also used to elicit in the reader subtle understandings that can only be approached indirectly. By placing words with an element that is metaphorically connected but not literally associated, the reader's creativity reaches, stretches, and then bridges a distance to an awareness that is new and not directly obvious. Thereby is achieved a special insight that is delicate and personal, something closer to intuition than explanation.

The words and the images resonate with each other the way the disparates of the world vibrate together in oneness. The tension that is generated in us by the differences we invent is an essential part of the creative process that finally leads to insight and resolution. This resolution is our necessary balance whether we are adventuring upon the sea, meeting the daily vicissitudes of common life, or merely reading/seeing this book.

Indeed, the subject of sailing and the images of bamboo, when placed together, are a constant reminder that an inner and deep-rooted balance is what we seek. We begin to find this balance when we understand that land and sea define each other, that one gives meaning and significance to the other. The very existence of one demands the other's existence. The apparent opposites of things balance each other. This balance finds and pervades us when we sense beyond differences and opposites, when the pieces of divided wholeness spontaneously meld together again.

Sea can only be balanced by land. A whole life fully embraces this duality, literally and metaphorically, because in body and thought we are creatures of both. Finally, we realize that we are both sea and land, both the sailboat sailing and the bamboo growing.

This realization is approached directly - not by arcane and supernatural powers, or by the mysterious and secret wisdom of ancient practices. It is not necessary that we employ occult or esoteric practices to consider the simple riddle of our being. It is enough that we are just here in the body of the Great Mother, breathing together with everything the common wholeness.

A harmonious wholeness requires sharing. Sharing yields to a need that is larger than our selfish interests, recognizes that there is something more than our separate and private willfulness. Taking is hard and aggressive, a getting by individual effort; sharing is soft and yielding, a receiving by general consent. Receiving requires a certain kind of compliance.

When we are able to meld compliance and volition, something unexpected and special happens. An easiness finds us. A grace pervades our being as we harmonize with the nature of things, as we move in concert with the Great Mother. We experience this easy grace, however, only when we have resolved the compliance/ volition paradox. Then, suddenly, there is no longer a difference between passive and active, between dependence and independence, between receiving and taking. And our sense of struggle falls away.

Struggle, perhaps, is our first conscious attempt at coming to terms with the whole we have divided into the separate parts of self and not-self. By putting together these divided parts, we mend this schism and discover a profound communion with things. Sailing is such a communion. Those who have sailed may know the mystical satisfaction, the exhilarating expansiveness that comes from being at one with wind and sea.

The sailboat itself is an image of this special way of being. It is resourceful, adaptive, silent. From the silence of its weight and shape comes a power that is peaceful and strong, serene and exciting, a belonging that does not trespass or counter the breathing wind and sea. So the ship moves in accord with the energy that is attendant, affirming itself and its harmony with the Great Mother. It has the presence of the Taoist sage, the sense of the Taoist way.

This sense is reflected in Lao Tzu's TAO TE CHING, written in China about the sixth century B.C. The words of the title literally mean, respectively, "the way the universe works", "virtue/power," and "classic/book". The image is one of having power by moving in accord with the way of things, and of having virtue by acting in harmony with the balanced way of the universe. Sailing, therefore, like Taoism, is a kind of existential judo, a t'ai chi of being in which surrounding energies are used only in compliance with the terms of themselves. Virtue/power [te] cannot be taken, it can only be received; the sailor can never take grace but may, by skill and sensitivity, discover how to receive it.

Virtue/power is not usually recognized because it is so obvious. To move by being blown is virtue/power. To use wind to sail into wind is virtue/power. To float is virtue/power. To be found by it and to know it is affirmation of our deepest belonging in the primal appropriateness of everything. We understand sailing as an expression of virtue/power simply because it has the same special ease and rightness.

When we sail, the energies of wind and sea are used and then returned unused; we go our way and the wind and sea continue as before. The process is profoundly ecological. We use yet do not use. With a quiet humility we enter nature's generosity and thereby receive the grace that is within the way of things.

So sailing is a spiritual experience because it enacts the primal harmony that is the very basis of our deepest knowing and belonging, because it enacts the inherent grace that is the nature of the Great Mother's vitality. The sailor who is close to wind and sea and ship is close to the Tao.

To be one with wind and sea and ship is to be one with the Tao. There are no mistakes in this kind of togetherness. Doing is guided by a deep empathy. Timing is exact. Struggle and effort become dance and play. A sailor then understands the sea like a sage understands the world. Outer energies are within so there is no need for inner resources. Like the sage, the sailor moves with the Tao and becomes virtue/power.

In virtue/power there is a fluidity and ease that comes from being in profound accord with nature's spontaneity (tzu jan). A sailboat moves with this spontaneity; its relationship with wind and sea is immediate and direct. Its response is thoughtless yet appropriate because what it is belongs where it is. It floats just-so in the sea; it heels just-so in the wind. Although the ship is unliving, it seems to be a thing alive. Thus it behaves as if it has an inner wisdom that enacts the effortless spontaneity of virtue/power.

Virtue/power is closely bound to the Taoist notion of not-doing (wu-wei) or doing-without-doing (wei-wu-wei). This is a special kind of not-doing that acknowledges the way of the universe and then, with deep empathy and without contrivance, acts in harmony with it. It means allowing what is rather than imposing what is not; it means accepting what naturally arises; it means not forcing; it means letting things do themselves.

Any effort to explain wu-wei will be immediately complicated by the inseparability of subject/object and thus cause/effect. While causal convention is used in Taoism, it is used as a means toward understanding beyond linear connectedness. Taoism, therefore, is a philosophy moving toward aesthetics, a science becoming art. Its disposition is to unify the divided psyche, to mend the schism between human and nature.

When we harmonize ourselves with nature, what is beneficial for one is beneficial for the other. When nature does of itself (tzu jan), we are fulfilled; when we practice wu-wei, nature is fulfilled. Wu-wei is the opposite of the West's tradition of acting upon nature.

The divided universe is a Western philosophical and religous convention that cannot be accepted if we are to understand wu-wei, Taoism, and the sailing/bamboo metaphors of this book. The notion that we are ***in here*** acting upon a universe ***out there*** is the illusion of separateness. We are in everything and everything is in us. Wu-wei, therefore, accounts for ourselves as an element in the unfolding of things, but in a joint way, as partners rather than masters. Wu-wei is like a ship floating or a sail filling; the ship just sits in water and the floating happens of itself, the sail just rises in wind and the filling happens of itself. With wu-wei, everything seems easy.

There is a propitiousness for doing everything - a time between now and later, a place between here and there - when things seem to do themselves. This is wu-wei. It is a way of going effortlessly and unobtrusively in the world. When nothing is taken and nothing is given, nothing is disturbed. Wu-wei is every event not obvious, every happening too harmonious and appropriate to be noticed. In short, it is what seems to occur easily and naturally of itself.

Beneath the apparent effortlessness of wu-wei and the practice of Taoism, however, there is a deeply sensitive empathy that synchronizes our individual will with the complexity and simultaneity of the way of things. This is a process not subject to simple linear explanation. If language is to explain Taoism, it will be in paradox and contradiction.

The linear form of language creates the illusion that things are explainable. Words create explanations that stretch in a sequential order of time and space. But explanations are like shorelines - after all their length and convolutions, they simply return to the beginning of themselves. All our explanations are islands. All our ingenuity merely defines itself. And beyond each shoreline is a vast expanse of wind and sea.

Words are the shorelines beyond which we cannot go with words. So the understanding we seek is not in words but in the unexplainable space beyond them. Words are our thoughts but the Tao cannot be thought. When we enter seaspace, we become other than words; we become moving wind and sea, an unchanging changing that stretches us beyond the shoreline's edge.

If we attend only to words, words will only be about words. But insight leaves us wordless, empty of explanation. Ultimately, THE TAO OF SAILING is not about words but about the space that surrounds them. Beyond all the shorelines of our words is the vastness of wind and sea.

When we open to wind and sea, wind blows through us and sea washes within us until we are changed. Then wind becomes the thoughts of our thinking and sea becomes the strength of our doing. When we return to land and words, we remain shoreless. With our minds, we think like wind; with our bodies, we do like sea.

Nothing is as confining as words; nothing is as expansive as the space they are within. In the vast moving of wind and sea, words are the places where we harbour and anchor, where we restrain the sailing of understanding and awareness.

This book uses words but its meaning lies beyond words. To be with the Tao, the wind and sea in which we so effortlessly move and float, we enter the horizons of what cannot be said. We look without words. We listen to silence. We let emptiness speak. And then we just drift free and hoist a sail.

THE TAO OF SAILING:

Shore

1. Even Beachstones

Even beachstones understand. They break and round with waves, become sand and nearly one with seaflow.

Yielding is the way of water. Water is the way of the Tao. But everything understands that holding fast against the way of things is futile. Even the hardness in stone knows water's way.

Be like water moving the way of the Tao. Or be like beachstones, breaking and rounding into flowing sand.

From birth until death's yielding, there is time enough to learn water's way.

2. The Wisdom Of Sand

Broken stones do not mend. But beachsand slowly fills behind a parting foot and parted waves form again after a ship's passing. The wisdom of sand is the hardness in stone that understands the way of water.

Be form moving toward the formless. Yield and overcome. Break and be whole.

The unchanging in everyone is a hardness that understands the wisdom of changing. This is why breaking becomes finding, and why losing has nothing to lose.

3. Neither Stone Nor Water

Neither stone nor water deviates from the way of the Tao. So the Tao is both hardness and softness. And something that is neither hardness nor softness.

Because of what it is, the Tao is everywhere and cannot be lost. Because of what it is not, the Tao is nowhere and cannot be found.

Therefore, the sage holds to what is and what is not, trusts in becoming and passing, attends to everything and nothing. Then finds without finding, does without doing, knows without understanding.

4. Words Say Stone And Water

Words say stone and water, so thoughts think hard and soft. But there are no words for what comes before words, no thoughts for what comes before thoughts.

In the silence before words are spoken and in the emptiness before thoughts are thought, there is something that cannot be said, that cannot be thought.

This is why words and thoughts are never quite enough.

5. Great Ocean...Dry Stones

Words say that great ocean combers shudder shore and tremble earth, that creeping tidewaves tickle dry stones wet. But words cannot say all that is between great and little, between still and moving, between wet and dry, between land and sea.

Silent wholeness is broken by a spoken word; whole stillness is shaken by a written word. Each word spoken undoes the spell of the unspoken; each word written undoes the spell of the unwritten. Be bound by words and miss the wordless wonder of things.

Word-bound is thought-bound. Be bound by words and think like words.

Words made of thoughts are thoughts made of words. So undo the doings of words.

6. Not Once A Mistake

The pattern of sand on open beaches, the order of water in churning tides, the rhythm of waves and the push of wind... at a glance, it seems as if the whole earth is thinking. Even its curve of horizons and shape of seas, its breathing seasons and quiet stones...and not once a mistake.

7. The Place Called Shore

On a sandy beach, where the land is soft and wide and changing, words say, "This is shore." On a sheer cliff, where the land is hard and narrow and unchanging, words say, "This is shore."

Where on the wide beach is the place called shore? Which moving grain of sand is shore? Or which space between which grains? Are tidepools shore? In the always changing of sand and sea, how can shore be found? Or is it hidden in the stillness of changing?

Where on the narrow seacliff is the place called shore? Is shore the thin wetness of sheer rock or is it the space between wet and dry, narrower than the narrowest, and so, no place at all? Or is it hidden in the stillness of unchanging?

In the wholeness of things, words are parts. If the way of parts is words, then the way of wholeness is silence. With just one word, break the silent stillness of unspoken wholeness, and the game of dividing begins.

Divide sea from land and then separate them with shore. This is how thoughts play themselves with tricks of words. But the Tao is neither words nor thoughts.

With awareness alert and indifferent, just softly and unthinkingly open. And there it is...without words that cannot explain, without thoughts that cannot understand.

8. If Shore Is Between

Everything could be easily explained if everything would come apart. Though thoughts try with words, there are never enough words, never enough thoughts.

If shore is between land and sea, what is between wet and dry, wave and water? What is between wind and sail, changing and unchanging, self and not-self? What is between words and thoughts?

Because each thing is more than itself, nothing that is, is only itself. This is why taking apart is never enough, and why explanations never quite explain.

9. Land And Sea, Here And There

Rise up! Declare for or against! Be a winner and a maker of losers.

Is the wind coming or going?

Divide the whole and there will be land and sea, here and there, this and that, one and other, right and wrong, good and bad, profit and loss, knower and known.

Birth and death define each other and then resolve each other. Call this: struggle within ease, adversity within grace, confusion within order, changing within stillness, something within nothing.

10. If There Is Land

That land should be land and sea should be sea seems so simple, until thoughts start asking questions. Are land and sea really different? Are differences really separate? Are land and sea separate and different from thoughts that think them? Can thoughts be trusted? Who decides?

Ask just one question and other questions appear from nowhere. This seems to be the way things happen. Take a side and suddenly there is another side. Find a self and instantly there is a not-self. Notice only one difference and then, as if by magic, there are differences everywhere.

This is how thoughts trick thoughts. If there is land then there must be sea. If there is this then there must be that. If there is knower then there must be known. If there is known then there must be unknown. If there is unknown then there must be questions. If there are questions then there must be answers. If there are answers then there must be questions. This is how questions and answers go in circles. When thoughts keep tricking themselves with thoughts, the Tao is found by thoughts thoughtlessly tricking themselves out of thoughts.

The Tao is the inner and outer way of everything. Thoughts thinking thoughts is the Tao. Thoughts tricking thoughts is the Tao. Even thoughts not thinking thoughts is the Tao. So never think and never not-think. This is why finding the Tao is so tricky.

11. Within The Reach Of Surf

Within the reach of surf, beachstones are changed to sand. In their changing, something does not change. In all changing, there is a stillness that does not change.

Waves move, but the sea itself is unmoved. In everything's changing, the changing itself is the stillness that remains the same.

Be the stillness in changing. Amid all changing, softly change until changing is a stillness. Become the stillness that is unchanging.

Unchanging is not the same as stillness. Be only the hardness of unchanging, and stillness will not be found; search for unchanging without stillness, and the Tao will not be found.

To find the Tao, first enter changing until it becomes unchanging. Then, enter unchanging until there is only stillness. Next, enter stillness until there is no longer even stillness.

Finally, rest full of empty.

12. Stone Thoughts

Water yields to stone and stone yields to water, so there is something more than hardness in stone, something more than softness in water.

If hardness was only hardness and softness was only softness, then everything would be simple to understand. But nothing fits understanding's simplicity.

Within every certainty there is something uncertain, so even the hardest thoughts searching for certainty finally admit uncertainty. Thinking finally convinces certainty to give up certainty.

Certainty is the hardness in thinking that yields to the softness of uncertainty.

In the softness of water, there is something harder than stone; in the softness of uncertainty, there is something deeply understood. Within every uncertainty there is something certain. The hardness in water cannot be found; the understanding in uncertainty cannot be explained.

Every thought is stone yielding to water or water yielding to stone. When stone thoughts become soft thoughts and water thoughts become hard thoughts, then uncertain thoughts begin to understand the Tao.

13. A Shoreless Thought

On land our limits are set by sea, and we must be watchful of shore. At sea our limits are set by land, and we must again be watchful of shore.

What is shore that it should separate land from sea and sea from land? What are thoughts that they should divide wholeness, and then with words, set one thing apart from another?

Divide wholeness with separate thoughts and then think shore to separate them. With words, assure their separation. Then thoughts that have separated thoughts from thoughts wonder and struggle with words and differences.

Without shore, with nothing to separate sea from land, what would divide wholeness?

What would be a wordless thought? What would be a shoreless thought? What would be the thoughtless whole?

14. Shoredance

The yielding of water identifies the hardness of stone; the motion of waves gives meaning to the stillness of rocks. One thing defines another.

But define one thing, find one difference, and suddenly there are differences everywhere. Then thoughts chase themselves in circles searching for what was before differences.

In the shoredance of waves and rocks, questions are always wrong, answers are never final, searching never ends.

To find a way that is other than waves and rocks, first choose one or the other. Then choose one and the other. Then choose neither. The sage chooses the shoreless shore.

In the shoredance of differences there is a still place that is without questions, without answers, without searching.

While thinking is searching with thoughts, stillness cannot be found. While understanding is searching with asking, wholeness cannot be found. Wholeness is unaware of differences and does not search.

When wholeness seems like emptiness and everything seems like nothing, then the shoredance of waves and rocks is finally stilled.

15. Between Land And Sea

There is something that seems stronger than strength, fuller than fullness, more lasting than unchanging. Unchanging seems to pass, and changing seems to endure. Fullness seems to be empty, and emptiness seems to be full. But no one knows why this is so.

Be hard and unyielding, be only unchanging, and the Tao seems to be soft and yielding and changing. Then strong thoughts cannot think it, ordered thoughts cannot understand it, determined thoughts cannot find it.

If the Tao was only soft and yielding and changing, then weak thoughts could think it, confused thoughts could understand it, lost thoughts could find it.

Between lost and found, between confusion and order, between weakness and strength, there is something that cannot be thought. Between yielding and unyielding, between changing and unchanging, between fullness and emptiness, there is something that cannot be understood. Between each word, there is something that cannot be said; between each thought, there is something that cannot be known.

Between land and sea there is something called shore, where opposites pass beyond opposites.

16. Master Of Nothing

Because wholeness binds together everything, each thing is of equal importance. A grain of sand is an entire beach. A seabird fills the whole sky. All the sea falls in a raindrop. The wholeness that binds together everything is each thing and all it does. It is the binding and the wholeness also.

The way of each thing and the way of everything is the way of the Tao. The greatest is least, and the least is greatest. Everything is the Tao, yet the Tao is nothing. Although the Tao is everywhere, it cannot be found. Nothing escapes it, yet nothing is bound by it. It is master of nothing, yet everything conforms to it.

Look for it...and it is nowhere. Look...and it is everywhere.

17. Stones Know What To Do

Stones know what do do. Water knows what to do. Even birds and fishes are not confused. But thoughts thinking about thoughts always get confused.

So return to the thoughtless beginning.

18. Beyond Land Is Sea

Beyond land is sea, and beyond sea is land. The circle game of words goes round and round forever.

Do not be dizzied by the turning of words. Between words there is a still place that is reached simply by forgetting words.

19. Closer To The Tao

Following is better than leading. Receiving is better than taking. Finding inner control is better than seizing outer control.

Therefore, follow the inner course and be led by an inner wisdom. By choosing what arises from the inside, move peacefully with the outside. Be guided by the inner source.

Yield like water finding its way. This is how the whole universe moves. Trust the downward course of things. Become the yielding that is everything's easiness.

Land can be landscaped, but sea cannot be seascaped. At sea we control less and so move closer to the Tao.

Ship

20. In The Full Middle

The sea below melds into the sky above; the sky above melds into the sea below. Only by remembered differences are sea and sky separate.

In the full middle, in both remembered sea and sky, is the sailboat, together with those together, united with those in union.

In the water of sea and the air of sky is the earth of ship and the fire of sailor, all together in a special togetherness.

21. Ships Are Not Mindful Of Sea

Ships are not mindful of sea, and sea is not mindful of ships, so floating does of itself. Sails are unaware of wind, and wind is unaware of sails so sailing does of itself.

When thinking is unaware of thinking then doing is unaware of doing, and things just do themselves.

Finding the Tao...is like losing the Tao. Knowing the Tao...is like forgetting the Tao.

22. The Form Of A Ship

Yielding is the way of water. So water yields, and heavy ships are easily floated.

When the form of a ship understands the formlessness of water, floating just happens. The ship itself does nothing but receive.

So the sage acknowledges doing but relies upon not-doing, attends to form but honours the formless. Thus, great things are easily accomplished.

23. Searching For A Way

A ship is hard and water is soft so they understand each other. Water is soft and rocks are hard so they understand each other. But a hard ship and hard rocks do not understand each other.

Near the hardness of rocks, the hardness of a ship moves through the softness of water, searching for a way; near the hardness of the world, we move the hardness of ourselves, searching for a way.

But there is a softness in the world that understands the hardness of our selves, until we find the softness of our not-selves. So, we make our way until the Way is found.

24. Between A Ship And Rocks

Between a sail and wind, between a hull and waves, there is an accord so that each can find its way with other. Between a ship and rocks there is sea so that hardness can find its way with hardness.

Between each thing there is the Tao so that everything can find its way with everything else.

The Tao is a special something that waits in stillness and arises in moving, a special accord that is used by everything but found by nothing. So no one knows what it is.

25. Just-So

Everything knows. Ship knows its shipness and does just-so. Rock knows its rockness and does just-so. Sea knows its seaness and does just-so.

With just-so, there cannot be blame if a ship meets rocks.

Searching through what and if, who and when, should and maybe, will not find the just-so of things. To find just-so, just empty of questions and searching, of excuses and explanations. Just-so is easiest to find as just-so.

26. An Anchor Too Heavy

An anchor too heavy cannot be lifted. A mast too high cannot be steadied. A sail too large cannot be tended.

More than enough is too much. Too much is less. Least is most.

27. Shaped For Sea And Wind

Ship and sail are shaped for sea and wind, but sea and wind are not shaped for ship and sail.

Because we act with purpose and the Tao acts without purpose, the Tao is found by giving up purpose. Without purpose, our doing arises from an inner wisdom, like the Tao arises from the Great Mother.

From the very beginning, the Great Mother has been nourishing everything, but no one can understand her purpose because everything is just the way it is.

A ship on the sea does not knowingly float; a sail in the wind does not knowingly fill. Waves and stones and clouds do not know what to do, yet never once do they make a mistake.

Give up purpose and never make a mistake. Become one with the Great Mother and arise from her wisdom.

28. That Which Moves A Ship

There is togetherness because there is separateness, and there is separateness because there is togetherness. And there is something other than separateness and together-ness that joins them together.

That which moves a ship upon the sea moves the sea beneath the ship and joins together the separate two.

The ship and the sea move together, separate in their togetherness and together in their separateness.

29. The Empty Space Within

The ancient sages taught that form comes from what is, but usefulness comes from what is not.

From the shape of a hull comes the form of a ship, but its usefulness comes from the empty space within.

A ship floats when its inner emptiness is within the sea. The sea is parted by what is, but the ship is floated by what is not. Because of what is not, what is, is made useful.

The is of things cannot be filled; the is-not of things cannot be emptied.

30. Both Lightness And Heaviness

A sailboat is built to float, and then its keel is weighted so it floats less.

Floating is not enough. Too light and a ship is not right with wind; too heavy and a ship is not right with sea.

For a special rightness with the world, both lightness and heaviness are needed.

31. Primal Harmony

A ship in moving swells rises and falls in thoughtless accord. With each changing swell, the ship changes in primal harmony.

Thoughts in a moving body do not consider, "When should I breathe in? When should I breathe out?" With the changing body, each breath thoughtlessly changes.

Breathe in and out as a ship rises and falls. Be ready as a ship is ready. Bend just-so with winds that blow. Move just-so with swells that move. Rest as a ship rests.

Best doing does not attend to its own doing.

32. Bow And Stern

Bow is with stern like coming is with going, like meeting is with parting, like beginning is with ending.

Following requires leading because leading requires following. Since bow and stern cannot be separated, one is not more than the other.

On a ship, bow and stern are easily recognized. Bow is for ahead: for forward motion, for great distances and destinations. Stern is for behind: for backward motion, for small distances and manoeuvering.

Bow is for meeting and dividing: where sea is whole and gives way, where inside and outside appear, where what is and what is not are made, where when meets now.

Stern is for leaving and joining: where sea is restored to whole, where inside and outside disappear, where what is and what is not are unmade, where now meets then.

The best bow makes no waves with its dividing. The best stern restores wholeness with its passing. The best moving leaves water undisturbed.

33. Without Being Minded

A proper ship tends to itself. In wind it balances without trying; in swells it rides without foundering. It sails without being minded.

A proper body tends to itself. In air it breathes without **deliberating**; in mountains it walks without stumbling. It moves without being minded.

34. Like An Old Sage

A sailboat that has inner wisdom is like an old sage. Quiet and ready and patient, it needs only a sailor's touch to awaken, to move, and to teach.

In the curve of its sails is the fullness of the world; in the strain of its rigging is the strength of the world; in the rush of its silence is the stillness of the world. In its heel…the wind is weighed; in its balance…the sea is danced; in its silence…the stillness is heard.

Within itself, the sailboat unknowingly knows. When, in timeless ease, the sailor becomes one with the ship, then oneness with the world is found.

To the ship, what words of gratitude can be spoken? How else but silently can a silent old sage be thanked?

35. A Ship's Oneness With Sea

The response of a ship to waves and wind is a special matter, for a sailor's oneness with sea must pass through the ship's oneness with sea.

To sail a ship that has a special rightness with sea is, indeed, a special fortune.

36. Whatness And Thatness

When a ship is heavy, it sits low in the water; when a ship is light, it sits high in the water. So ship and water understand each other.

This we can understand as the whatness of things. But we cannot understand the thatness of things.

Whatness and thatness are different. Whatness comes from what is - from the substantial and manifest; thatness comes from what is not - from the formless and hidden. Whatness is the invented explanation; thatness is the discovered mystery.

Without one thought of whatness...go directly to thatness! Without listening, open ears and hear! Without looking, open eyes and see!

Remember only the whatness of things, and the Tao will never be found.

37. In Its Very Centre

A sailboat understands the Tao. It heels to port, it heels to starboard. But always in its very centre is an inner balance.

38. Perfect Balance

The shape of a ship does not change to meet changing waves; the balance of a ship does not change to meet changing winds. Without changing, differences are accounted for.

Somewhere within a ship, something unchanging accounts for changing; somewhere inside there is a something that is the same yet never-the-same, a balanced stillness that understands waves and winds the way we try to understand the world.

When the outer is always changing, then understand with inner stillness. If the shape of a ship can understand the sea, how easily then can the shapelessness of thoughts understand the world.

Deliberation stiffens and anticipation limits. But the readiness of inner stillness always waits with perfect balance.

With the Tao, everything is accounted for. But no one knows how.

39. The Wing Of Sail

The wing of sail divides wind and then joins it together again. Nothing is used, so nothing is wasted. Nothing is taken, so nothing is returned. Nothing is done, yet things are not the same. This is doing without doing. Such is the way of the sage.

The sage seems to do nothing yet great things are accomplished. Because receiving is valued above taking and following is honoured above leading, the world goes its proper way. Nothing is disturbed, so everything fulfills itself.

This is the way of the Tao. It neither does nor does not do. Though nothing, it is in everything. Because of it, each thing moves in its proper course. Invisible yet present, hidden yet everywhere, it is lost when found and found when lost.

40. Holding And Yielding

The holding in a sail shapes wind; the yielding in a sail is shaped by wind.

Holding holds until yielding is just right; yielding yields until holding is just right.

Too tight and effort is wasted; too loose and nothing is accomplished.

41. The Balance Within

A sailboat in wind steadies itself. When the steadiness comes from the balance within, the direction of wind does not matter.

With inner balance there is readiness without preparation, response without deliberation.

Coming as the best or coming as the worst, everything is treated as the same.

42. Silent Sound And Sounding Silence

With silent sound and sounding silence a sailboat moves through wind and sea.

The water and windsounds of sailing arise from silence and then return to silence. Silence is the beginning and the end of every sound. Every sound echoes in silence.

A silent ship is the sound of the full silence that pervades everything.

What more can be said than the fullness of silence? What could be greater than the silent echo of silence?

43. A Moving Stillness

A sailboat moves, but nothing upon it moves. By using what is given, it moves without moving.

Shaped for wind and sea, it is one with moving; shaped from earth and stone, it is one with stillness.

In this world only a sage moves with a moving stillness.

44. Unmoved Yet Moving

A becalmed ship, its sails draped in hanging air, is unmoved in the stillness of sea. Then air releases, sea changes, and the ship moves.

In the moving wind and waves there still remains the stillness of the ship, unmoved yet moving, not doing, yet somehow doing. And out of a stillness that moves, sailing just silently happens.

When inner stillness is unmoved by outer changing, then there is proper doing. Out of a stillness - like a ship is in sea, like a sail is in wind - doing just silently happens.

45. The Ship's Cockroach

By itself alone a hull cannot float, a rudder cannot steer, a sail cannot move a ship. One thing requires another. Another requires more. More requires many. Many requires the All. This is why there is only the Tao.

Thoughts searching for the Tao find nothing. Thoughts searching for nothing find...wetness of sea, scale of fish, rounding of beach-stones.

So search for the greatest by returning to the least. Begin with the common and end with the ordinary. This is how small thoughts become large enough to find the Tao.

Better still, forget the Tao and honour the ship's cockroach.

46. The Same Mystery

Whether there is one fathom beneath a keel or one thousand fathoms, the same mystery floats a ship. Different waves, yet one sea; different everything, yet one Tao.

When searching for the Tao, there is no difference between one and many, between same and different.

47. Timing

Ships in swells know when to rise and fall. Waterdrops on sails know when to release. Seaspray knows when to return to sea. Clouds know when to rain.

Too early and there will be urging. Too late and there will be restraining.

When inner and outer arise together, the timing will be correct. Then things just do themselves...as if no one is doing and nothing is being done.

48. A Ship Is Woman

To a sailor, a ship is woman because it holds and enfolds. To a ship, the sea is woman because it holds and enfolds.

To the sea, the earth is woman because it holds and enfolds.

To the earth, the great void is woman because it holds and enfolds.

This is how the Great Mother is - how she holds within holding and how she holds without holding.

49. Like Sails

Sails rise into air for wind, and when wind comes, they fill full. Wait in patience and receive. With little...fill full. With too much...empty.

Change shape but be unchanged...like sails.

50. By Not Surpassing

A sailboat arises from earth and fire but belongs with air and water.

From its belonging comes its moving and from its moving comes its belonging.

It moves with moving wind and sea but is never more than wind and sea. From their moving comes its moving, so what it does arises from what they do. Its moving is its belonging, and its belonging is its moving.

From belonging comes accord. When there is accord, inner doing becomes outer harmony.

When inner and outer move together, there cannot be surpassing. Without surpassing, the strength of the inner becomes the fulfillment of the outer. Thus, more arises from less, and power and virtue become one.

51. Everything And Nothing

A ship must mean everything and a ship must mean nothing. Everything and nothing. Valuable and useless. Choose both.

Then neither.

52. Moon Floats...Ship Floats

The moon floats and the ship floats. The laws are called different, but the mystery is the same. The accord of a ship with the sea is the same as the accord of the moon with the earth, the earth with the stars, the stars with the more, the more with the All.

Ship and sea and moon and earth and stars...there are smaller mysteries, and there are larger mysteries, but all mysteries are the same mystery. All explanations still leave something unexplained. There is more to mystery than explaining can explain.

Beyond each known is the next unknown. Beyond each unknown is the same mystery.

Name the mystery. Call the mystery wonder. Call the wonder nameless. Call the nameless the Tao. Words are not enough.

53. Stillness And Emptiness

When wind and sail come together, a ship is moved by something that is neither wind nor sail; when water and hull come together, a ship is floated by something that is neither water nor hull.

Between the different things of the world, there is something that is not a thing; between the opposites of the world, there is something that is not an opposite. But no one knows what it is because it is neither one thing nor another.

What moves is known by what is still; what is full is known by what is empty; what is, is known by what is not. So not everything can be known.

Most people attend to what can be known. But the sage attends to what cannot be known, and, thereby, moves with stillness and emptiness through the things and opposites of the world.

54. Being Sea...Being Waves

Sea does not attend to being sea; waves do not attend to being waves.

Thoughts cannot understand themselves when examining themselves. Thinking cannot know itself when pondering itself. We cannot be ourselves when considering ourselves.

Not even the Tao is aware of itself. This is why searching will never find the Tao.

55. The Sea Of Ourselves

We think peaceful and we think stormy, so the peaceful sea and the stormy sea is the sea of ourselves.

Is the sea kind? Is the sea cruel? This is the sea of ourselves, the sea of our own thinking and feeling and making.

We are ourselves and the sea is itself, separately together, divided by wholeness.

Thoughtlessly and selflessly, then, what is sea?

56. The Stillness Of Sea

In the sound of waves is the silence of sea; in the changing waves is the stillness of sea.

When silence fills sound and stillness fills changing, then emptiness fills understanding and the Tao finds itself.

57. Sea And Fog

Sea and fog...water silently becoming air...air silently becoming water.

58. Thoughts Of Waves... Thoughts Of Sea

Who would separate waves from sea and say, "These are waves but this is sea." Yet thoughts of waves forget thoughts of sea.

Thoughts separate wholeness into parts and then forget wholeness. Waves and sea are separate only in thoughts that have separated one thing from another and then have forgotten the separating.

To return to the Tao, remember thoughtless wholeness.

59. When A Wave Comes

When a wave comes, do not say, "This alone is wave." The wave comes from wind, from the shoal of bottom, the flow of tides, the expanse of sea...

The wave comes from all things. All things come from all other things. So it is that each thing is everything . . . all at once.

60. In One Grey

Sea meets sky and sky meets sea...in one grey.

Only by habit do smaller thoughts remember the separateness of things.

61. Wordless Sea

Without a thought of sea, without a thought of seeing, leave sea unchanged by thoughts.

Thoughtlessly and selflessly, with no one looking and no one seeing, let sea happen in the inside of emptiness.

When thoughts are still and the inside of seeing is empty, be filled with wordless sea.

62. On The Sea's Surface

On the sea's surface, reflected wholes are broken into parts. When are wholes not broken into parts? When are thoughts still enough to understand the wholeness of things?

63. Before Spray Returns To Sea

Before spray returns to sea, is it part of sea? Before rain returns to sea, is it part of sea? When does rain become sea and sea become rain? Is wind that makes waves a part of sea? Is sea that makes fog a part of sky?

Divided thoughts try to understand the undivided everything; unchanging thoughts try to understand the changing everything. How can the parts of unchanging thoughts understand the whole of everything's changing?

When the unchanging of divided thoughts gets tired of trying, then understanding arises from the stillness of empty thoughts.

With still thoughts, understand everything's changing; with empty thoughts, understand everything's wholeness.

64. Sea Belongs With Land

The belonging of each thing is assured by every other thing. Sea belongs with land, waves belong with wind, fish belong with water. In all the Great Mother, there is nothing not useful, not used.

The sameness and difference of each thing makes everything belong just-so.

Even not-belonging belongs. If not-belonging did not belong, the Great Mother would stop breathing.

65. The Wave Unknowingly

In a moving wave, stillness cannot be seen; in the changing world, the Tao cannot be understood.

The stillness of the Tao can only be found when thoughts are still enough to enter the world's changing.

When still thoughts enter changing, they become changing thoughts that change in stillness. This is entering the wave without stopping the wave, entering the world without stopping the world.

When the wave and the world are entered, changing becomes still. This is how the wave unknowingly moves in accord with the sea, and how the sage unknowingly moves in accord with the world.

66. The Water Of Waves

The water of waves rises from trough to crest and then returns from crest to trough. Windborne spray flies from sea to air and then returns from air to sea.

So it is that everything returns to its rightful place.

67. Deep Within The Sea

Deep within the sea, there is a stillness that is like the beginning of everything's changing. Even before anything changed, changing waited in stillness.

In waiting stillness, something moved and changed and became. From stillness and unchanging came becoming, and then one thing, and then another, and then everything.

Because everything came from one thing and changing came from stillness, stillness is still in changing and oneness is still in everything. So, through oneness and stillness, anyone can find the Way.

Attend to the beginning of the beginning. It still waits in everything as a stillness in changing's deep silence.

68. Different Waves

Different waves, yet one sea; different things, yet one Great Mother.

Different winds and clouds and seasons, yet just one Tao.

69. The Pathless Path

The sea is pathless because it is all path. Find a path on the pathless path.

This is how all can be none and how none can be all. And this is why the Tao is so easy and so difficult to find.

The obvious is hidden; the conspicuous is invisible. This is just the way things are. The Tao is everywhere, but no one knows what it is.

Because no one can leave the pathless path, even our simplest questions cannot be answered.

70. The Wholeness Of Sea

Seaspray returning to sea disappears into the wholeness of sea. All the separate parts of things disappear into the wholeness of the Great Mother. So the sage notices parts but attends to wholeness.

The wholeness of the Great Mother arises out of the emptiness within herself. So the sage notices the Great Mother but attends to emptiness.

From wholeness comes the wisdom of the Great Mother; from emptiness comes the Way of the Great Mother.

71. Upon the Sea Of The Great Mother

Our thoughts float in ships of words upon the sea of the Great Mother. They play upon her surface, heedless of the dark silence beneath.

From deep in the dark silence, an emptiness summons us out of words and thoughts. Listen to this inner silence. It is the sound of emptiness.

The deep emptiness is the womb of the Great Mother, the dark beginning of the beginning. Just beneath our every word and thought...it waits. Listen to its silence. Answer with silence. And then sink with emptiness into emptiness and be received.

72. Particular Gratitude

When wind blows, can sails be thanked for their filling? And how can wind be thanked? When rain falls, can clouds be thanked for their wetness? And how can rain be thanked? When stars or moon or sun reflect on sea, how can sea be thanked?

When everything happens because of everything else, when each thing is because of all other things, how can there be particular gratitude?

73. Shapeless, Formless, Nameless

Wave is only called wave. Wind is only called wind. Sea is only called sea. Names are given and then the naming is mistaken for the knowing.

Naming is a stopping. Without naming, there is no stopping. Who would stop a wave to know a wave?

Without stopping, something is kept that would otherwise be lost. Without naming, there is nameless wave.

Things are not the shape of names; the shape of names is not the knowing. When there is not-naming, something is known that is shapeless, formless, nameless.

74. Softer Than Water

The nature of sea is water, and the nature of water is yielding.

Within yielding is the beginning of unyielding. Thus, it is said, yielding that only yields is unyielding.

Hold only to yielding and hardness will arise; hold only to unyielding and softness will arise. Within water is the beginning of stone; within stone is the beginning of water. Water finally crumbles and stone finally flows. Yielding or unyielding is not enough.

To find the Tao...be unyielding while yielding, and be yielding while unyielding. Be harder than stone, softer than water.

75. Because Of Awe

Because of awe, a drop of water is as great as the vastness of sea. Because of awe, each mystery is the same mystery. Awe reveals the common mystery in everything.

The common mystery in everything is ordinary.

76. The Sea Remains

T hough changed by moon and sun and wind, the sea itself remains unchanged.

Each thing is changed by what is not itself, yet each thing does nothing but be itself.

Although we are changed by what is not ourselves, we do nothing but be ourselves. We are ourselves and not-**ourselves.** Inner and outer are the same. Is and is-not are one.

With nothing to do or change, suddenly, everything is easy.

77. Only Sea Meeting Sky

O nly sea meeting sky.

In the west...sets a round, full sun. In the east...rises a round, full moon.

What is here in the full middle that thoughts cannot understand? What are thoughts that they cannot dispel awe in the heart?

Between the fullness of sun and moon, there is the Tao. Between the fullness of everything, there is a special something that thoughts cannot quite remember, that the heart cannot quite forget.

78. To Be Unmastered

The way of water is special. That which changes cannot be lost. That which yields cannot be broken. That which breaks cannot be destroyed.

How easy, then, to be unmastered.

79. The Stillness In Everything's Moving

Find a ship and it moves. Find a wave and it moves...even the great seas and the simple stone and the dancing continents. From one thing to another, from least to greatest, everything moves with everything else. The way of this moving is called the Tao. This is why everything changes and nothing is ever the same.

In everything's moving, within the moving itself, there is a stillness that does not move. The way of this stillness is also called the Tao. This is why everything changes yet nothing is ever different.

Whether moving or still, everything belongs within the Great Mother. She nurtures everything by letting all things be.

The moving in everything's stillness is the Great Mother's vitality. The stillness in everything's moving is the Great Mother's allowing.

80. Below The Sea's Surface

How did the great sea and the flying birds and the wonderful sky come to be? Who can know? How can one small mind understand the beginning of the huge and many?

And yet, when thoughts dive through thoughts, something deep in the belly seems to know. When eyes search down and down, deep below the surface of the sea, something seems to wait in the depth and darkness and silence.

From the vast and easy weight of sea, there must have come a primal urge, a beginning before the beginning, a something between nothing and the first something, a knowing before there were even thoughts.

81. What Could Be Easier

Without desiring, without wishing, without even wanting, the Tao just is. By neither seeking nor by not seeking, by neither thinking nor by not thinking, it still is.

Unattended...waves move, fishes swim, birds fly. What could be easier?

Sailor

海員

82. Thoughts Within Thinking

Thoughts within thinking pass like waves beneath a ship. And just when they arrive, they leave.

So it is that, moment by moment, we rise and fall on the great circle of our years, somehow learning an inner balance.

83. How Are We To Be In This World

How can winds that blow upon sea, not make waves? How can ships that move upon sea, not disturb water?

How are we to be in this world so that things are left as themselves?

84. The Bending Course

When the sea is hardened by the strength of a storm, a sailboat's heeling softens to the rising winds, and the ship's moving yields to the rising waves.

By softening and yielding, we acknowledge the strength of the world; by hardening and resisting, we acknowledge the strength of ourselves.

This is why the Tao is found by both yielding and resisting, and why the bending course of a strong sailor will not break.

85. Defiance...Yielding...Accord

For a sailor at sea, defiance acknowledges the Tao, yielding finds the Tao, accord confirms the Tao.

86. Fullness In Waiting

While waiting...move like the sea. Find fullness in waiting.

87. Thoughtless Accord

Feet are not mindful of legs. Arms are not mindful of body. Thoughts are not mindful of mind.

In thoughtless accord a sailboat falls and then rises in swells, heels and then straightens in winds.

In all the workings of the world, everything is thoughtlessly in accord with everything else. This is how still is with moving, how greatest is with least, how one is with another. To become one with the world, thoughtlessly attune to the world.

When thinking...not one thought of what to think. When doing...not one consideration of what to do. When being...not one idea of what to be.

This is how the sage joins the inner with the outer, and becomes one with the world.

88. Surprise And Uncertainty

Seeing sea is inner meeting outer, nothing meeting something. In such a meeting, who knows what to expect - so surprise. In such a meeting, which is sea and which is seeing - so uncertainty.

Surprise and uncertainty - a propitious beginning.

89. Thinking Is Difficult To Find

Waves move, but the sea itself is unmoved. Air moves, but the wind itself is unmoved. The shape of a sail changes, but the sail itself is unchanged.

Like seawinds, thoughts change, but thinking never changes.

Thoughts are easy to find because of their changing; thinking is difficult to find because of its unchanging.

90. Within The Wind Of Thinking

A wind blowing across the sea does not empty of itself and become less than wind. Though never the same air, it remains the same wind. Within its blowing, there is a stillness that does not change with changing.

Within everything, there is a stillness that does not change with changing.

Within the wind of thinking, find the stillness that does not change when thoughts change.

91. The Silence of Emptiness

For a sailor, enclosed and afloat on a ship, the ship is called female. For a ship, enclosed and afloat on the sea, the ship is called male.

For those who play with words, each thing is more than there are words to call it. There are never enough words to name everything that anything is.

Because so many words are still not enough words, name things wordlessly. Then, without words, hear the silence of emptiness.

Silence is the emptiness that pervades everything. Each thing is named by an inner silence, heard by an outer silence.

92. The Losing Of Self

Sea is not just sea. Sail is not just sail. Ship is not just ship. There is not one thing that is only itself. Be only one thing and lose something important; be all things and find something important.

The finding of self is a losing; the losing of self is a finding.

93. The Sage's Thoughts

Like seawinds, the sage's thoughts blow quite beyond control.

94. Inner Weight

A ship heels in winds and sails well because it has inner weight.

With inner weight, we yield to the way of things and move just-so in the winds of the world.

When inner weight has been found, trust its deep and constant balance. From this centre that no one can explain, the difficult is made easy and adversity is mastered. But no one knows how.

95. Balanced Moving

Winds move waves, waves move ships, and ships move sailors. Waves do not hold fast against winds, ships do not hold fast against waves, sailors do not hold fast against ships.

In all matters, do not hold fast.

A balanced ship, moving in balance with waves, teaches balance. When a sailor moves with the ship's moving and finds at its very centre its balanced stillness, this is the beginning of the sailor's balanced moving with everything's moving.

96. Let Finding Find Its Own Way

Wholeness is thoughtlessly itself. The Tao is the thoughtless way of wholeness. Who knows why everything is the way it is? Who can explain wholeness? Who can get outside everything to understand the inside of it? So, understand the Tao from the inside.

Begin with the way of water. Instead of shaping everything to understanding, let understanding take the shape of everything. Be ready and easy. Without even knowing or wanting to know, follow the inner course.

Without one idea, let thinking think; without one explanation, let finding find its own way.

97. No One Doing...Nothing Being Done

Struggle is created when waves are separated from winds and when self is separated from not-self. Try to separate a ship from sea or a sail from wind, and trouble begins. A sailor who divides the world, struggles with the world.

When distinctions disappear, the world is whole and struggles cease. With no one doing and nothing being done, sailing just happens.

Thus, when a great sea has been crossed, there is no one to take credit, no one to receive praise.

98. Proper Yielding

The sailor yields to the moving ship; the ship yields to the moving sea; the sea yields to the moving All.

Since least is affected by greatest, and greatest is affected by least, be greatest and least.

When yielding, yield as both greatest and least. Then, there is proper yielding.

99. The Sailor's Task

Within hardness is the beginning of softness, and within softness is the beginning of hardness. So, wordlessly and thoughtlessly, the softness of sea and the hardness of ship understand each other.

The sailor's task is to understand both hardness and softness and to comply with the understanding between ship and sea.

100. Our Moving Thoughts

Our moving blood knows waves. Our moving breath knows wind. Our moving body knows sea.

How easy, then, for our moving thoughts to know the Tao.

101. Simplicity

The more the body is adorned, the more its essence is concealed; the more luxurious a sailboat, the more its sailor is hidden. Find a simple ship and the sailor is most apparent.

The more that is added, the less there is.

When enough is enough, more is too much.

102. Unmade-Up Mind

Wind blows in one direction, but we want to go in another; wind blows there, but we want to stay here. Wind keeps getting in the way of made-up mind.

So...change made-up mind to unmade-up mind.

103. Thoughts Are Like Waves

Thoughts thinking about sea think that sea and thoughts about sea are different. Why? Because thoughts don't trust thoughts.

Why don't thoughts trust thoughts? Because they don't understand themselves. And why don't they understand themselves? Because they follow themselves in circles. And they follow themselves in circles because they have neither wholeness nor silence nor stillness.

Now, this thought about thoughts has just thought something important, but it cannot be explained without going in circles.

Only when thoughts stop explaining thoughts to thoughts with more thoughts do thoughts become clear.

Thoughts are like waves and thinking is like sea - thoughts cannot understand thinking and thinking cannot explain thoughts.

104. Yield And Be Unbroken

Unyielding ships are broken by waves; unyielding people are broken by circumstances.

Therefore, move as a sailboat moves. Go quietly. Stay balanced. Comply with the way of things. Take the sea's time. Be neither forceful nor devious. With the gentle...be gentle. Bend to the powerful...give way to the overpowering. Yield and be unbroken. Be unbroken and be whole.

Wholeness understands that inner and outer are one, that self and not-self arise from each other and are the same. This is why nothing is lost by yielding and why nothing is gained by not yielding.

This is why the sage can yield without yielding.

105. Right Questions

When questions are wrong, answers are difficult to find. Right answers first require right questions.

Rain meeting sea...water meeting water. What could be the use? What could be the meaning?

Does the sea get wet in the rain?

In the vast world, how do we find our way? In the vast sea, how does a fish find its way?

106. Inner Patience

Inner patience begins when there is no longer waiting in waiting-for-wind. From inner patience comes outer patience. This is how softness in the heart overcomes hardness in the world.

When we soften to wind and waiting, moving is without hurry, passing is without time.

When the heart becomes timeless, an inner softness balances the world.

107. Selfless Changing

At anchor, stopping tends to itself; at sea, going tends to itself. Stopping is easy when we are stopped; going is easy when we are going. But when do we stop when we are going, and when do we go when we are stopped? Changing is difficult.

Difficulty comes from attachment. Without attachment, everywhere is treated as the same. When everywhere is the same, stopping and going are the same. Without differences, nothing changes. When nothing changes, there is nothing to decide. When there is nothing to decide, no one decides.

No one deciding is selfless changing. Selfless changing is the changing emptiness between stopping and going, between all the opposites of made-up mind.

108. A Sailor At Sea

A sailor at sea is away from land and closer to the Tao. Land cannot be possessed so it is understood; sea cannot be controlled so it is honoured.

In the vastness of sea, belonging is nowhere so finding is everywhere. In the timelessness of sea, planning is unnecessary so doing just happens of itself. In the solitude of sea, propriety and morality are not needed so the inner course is opened. Thus, virtue and power arise from the primal source.

The less needed, the more attained. No needs, so no discontent. No discontent, so no desires. No desires, so no misfortune. No misfortune, so the inner balance is found.

When there is inner balance, nothing can be lost and nothing can be gained. This is the emptiness that is full, the fullness that is empty.

But it is not the way of most people.

109. Words Are Like Air

Words are like air...look through them but not at them. Words are not the same as seeing.

Call a fish what we will, we have no word for what it calls itself.

110. Wave And Self

From unchanging arises changing, and from changing arises unchanging.

From the unchanging sea comes the changing wave; from the unchanging Tao comes the changing self.

Wave and self are their changing, so do not think, "This is wave!" or "This is self!" Wave and self do not even stop for thoughts.

Without thoughts, let changing change. When wave falls away and not even self remains, then changing becomes the unchanging Tao.

111. Neither Thoughts Nor Understanding

Water reflects like thoughts understand. Seek the still water that does not disturb reflecting; seek the still thoughts that do not disturb understanding.

Seek patiently and gently so the seeking does not disturb the water. Thoughts desperately searching for understanding find only confusion.

The Tao cannot be found by searching, so leave thoughts undisturbed. In undisturbed thoughts there is a stillness that is the beginning of understanding.

112. A Sailor's Course At Sea

A sailor's course at sea accounts for winds and currents. When winds and currents come from behind, the course is direct; when winds and currents come from ahead, the course is indirect. The direct course is not hurried; the indirect course is not devious. In all the winds and currents of the world, be neither hurried nor devious.

By taking the world's time and honouring the world's course, the sage lives harmoniously with the world. Sometimes this is seen as a special grace, sometimes as a special power.

When distant destinations are reached or great things are accomplished, they are done by neither grace nor power. But by something else.

113. The Mysterious Ordinary

The Tao is the unknowable way of the mysterious ordinary. All things are related by a common mystery that pervades everything.

Beyond words and thoughts and understanding, all wonder is the same wonder, all awe is the same awe.

114. Names...Thoughts

Since the Tao is only called the Tao, any name should do. But choose a name and it seems too grand or too paltry, too vague or too confining, too serious or too foolish. This is the way with names...they try but never succeed.

Names cannot capture what is other than names; thoughts cannot think what is other than thoughts.

So...be silent when naming, be thoughtless when understanding.

115. Every New Journey

Sail far enough and the Great Mother's wisdom returns us to the beginning. Leaving has always been the beginning of returning.

All goings are comings. All our journeys return us to the beginning that we did not recognize.

When the beginning is recognized, there are no new endings. Then, from a still place in every new leaving, every new journey is familiar.

116. Breath And Blood...Air And Water

The easy moving of wind and waves churns seas and strains sails, heaves ships and shapes continents. By easy moving, great things are easily accomplished.

The easy moving of breath and blood is the living air and water of our vitality, the inner urging that moves the hardness and stillness of bones and flesh to great accomplishments.

Move easily in the world. Be yielding and soft, humble and bending. Change but be unchanged. Attend to everything's belonging. Respect the least as if it is the greatest. Use what circumstances provide. Avoid both inner confidence and outer show. Cultivate timelessness. Honour the way of the Great Mother. Like the Tao, be with everything, yet meddle with nothing.

117. Nothing In Charge

The sun does not knowingly make the day. The earth does not knowingly turn in seasons. The sea does not knowingly reflect the moon.

In giving, in taking, in receiving...leave nothing in charge.

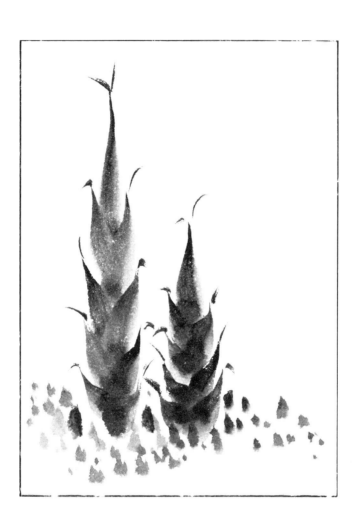

118. Inner Balance...Outer Harmony

Struggle against becalmed, and the waiting becomes long; struggle against storms, and the forces become great.

Resistance is the beginning of opposition; contention is the beginning of hostility; struggle is the beginning of adversity.

When the inner knows how to enter the outer, the world is left as it is. Then the long seems short, the difficult seems easy, the extraordinary seems ordinary.

Outer harmony arises from the stillness of inner balance. So no trouble. Not even wonder.

119. As Large As Nothing

With fullness within, become as large as sea being held in the roundness of earth.

With roundness within, become as large as earth being held in the vastness of emptiness.

With emptiness within, become as large as nothing holding everything.

120. The Primal Urge

The primal urge is everywhere: in the moving air and the nestling sea, even in the sailing ship and the waiting stone. It is everywhere but found nowhere.

Inside, it is a silent breathing that fills each thing with its own self. Outside, it is a silent wind that blows each thing in its own way.

Become the breathing wind of the primal urge. Though silent and invisible, it is ever present. Find what cannot be found.

Use and be used. Use what cannot be found; be used by what cannot be known.

Arise from the inner mystery and move with the outer mystery. Become fulfillment fulfilling itself.

121. Only Night And Sea And Fog

Only night and sea and fog.
   In the black and silence and stillness, nothing moves, nothing is.

No place to be in, to come from, to go to.

In this no-place there is...empty fullness, full emptiness.

122. By Moving with Everything

For all its expanse and great weight, the sea is held in confinement by land, blown in disarray by wind, even bound in conduct by the nature of itself.

The master of a ship is bondsman to the puff of wind and servant to the grain of rice.

Because the least endures and the lowest overcomes, those who follow the Tao are followed by the Tao.

By moving with everything...move everything. Tighten the sheet and pull in the sky. Take the helm and steer the stars.

123. Rest Full Of Empty

On the great rounded sea, a moving ship does not hold to straight. In all matters, do not hold to straight.

First find soft curves. Then find greater curves.

Let curves enlarge to roundness. Then let roundness enlarge until nothing is beyond roundness.

Take away outside. Take away inside.

Rest full of empty.

124. Timeless Waiting

When the sea is silent, and becalmed ships drift aimlessly, wind cannot be summoned. But, in timeless waiting, wind summons itself.

When seaspray flies from blown waves, and ships heave to or hide in harbours, wind cannot be subdued. But, in timeless waiting, wind subdues itself.

Become less than doing, less than purpose, less than silence. Then there is timeless waiting.

In timeless waiting, no one waits. When self and not-self are the same, when there is only the timeless Tao thoughtlessly not-doing, then everything arrives on time.

125. Changing Thoughts

Let thoughts change as wind and waves change. Do not try to hold thoughts unchanged. How can unchanging thoughts understand everything's changing?

Let changing thoughts take the shape of understanding, like changing wind and waves take their proper shape.

When thoughts change, let them change in stillness so their changing does not disturb the changing.

126. Practice Not-Doing

Waves and seasons, days and generations, rise and fall in easy rhythms. In the Great Mother's allowing, there is an inner wisdom that guides the natural course of things. When the Great Mother is honoured, a balanced changing moves in everything.

In the affairs of people, when they do not honour the inner wisdom of things, too much creates even more, not enough creates even less, and those with big solutions just create bigger problems.

Trust the Great Mother and leave things undone. Practice not-doing. Let the easy order of things arise from her wisdom. The less done, the less disturbed.

Thus, it is said, "When the emperor does not rule, there is peace in the kingdom."

127. Their Own Horizons

Where is the one thought that is all thoughts? Where are still thoughts at rest?

Is there a mast high enough to climb where thoughts can view their own horizons and see the roundness of themselves curving back to themselves?

128. A Special Waiting

When winds do not blow and sails do not fill, ships do not move. For sailors, this is a special waiting called becalmed. It is a special not-happening, a special not-doing, a special stillness in which something unknowable moves.

Out of stillness arises moving; out of least arises greatest; out of nothing arises something. In the stillness between winds...something moves; in the stillness between thoughts...something is understood. This special something is most apparent in stillness.

Be patient and easy and ready. Then receive what is waiting.

129. Less Than What Is Not

The Tao cannot be found without taking into account all the stars, one drop of sea, and even this silly self.

In all of heaven and earth, there is room enough for both self and not-self, space enough for both everything and nothing. So the Tao is more than what is, and less than what is not.

130. An Emptiness Makes Way

In the sea, water yields and an emptiness makes way for ships. In the wind, air yields and an emptiness makes way for sails. In everyone, something yields and an emptiness makes way for the Tao.

131. Just Sitting

Unattended...waves break on shores...winds blow...clouds move. No trouble. No bother. Not even effort.

Just sitting...merely holding the helm...winds fill sails and the ship moves itself.

132. Wind-Knowing

When understanding grows greater and greater, and blows beyond thoughts and self, it becomes wind-knowing...formless and everywhere.

ABOUT THE ARTIST - WILLIAM GAETZ

William Gaetz was born in Victoria, British Columbia, in 1934. An accomplished vocalist and concert pianist, Mr. Gaetz has long been a student of philosophy and religion, concentrating his intellectual energies on Zen and metaphysics. After years of expressing his creativity professionally through photography, he embarked on the path of Chinese brush painting under the tutelage of Master Professor Peng Kung Yi. It is a medium that Mr. Gaetz feels best fulfills his artistic needs.

In 1988, as a consequence a public showing of his brush paintings, Mr. Gaetz was asked to illustrate THE TAO OF BEING: A THINK AND DO WORKBOOK, a challenge he met admirably. The following year his talents were summoned to illustrate THE TAO OF SAILING.

The challenge was formidable because the book is and is not about sailing. How could the illustrations respect this inherent paradox? Representational drawings were too confining and photographs were too depictive for a book that was meant to be understood both literally and metaphorically. Mr. Gaetz suggested bamboo. Bamboo was exactly right.

Using a single bamboo theme and a process of creative association, he has invented a wide range of subtle moods that reflect and enhance the book's chapters. His images have the same spontaneity and appropriateness that recall the natural and intuitive character of Taoism itself.

ABOUT THE AUTHOR - RAY GRIGG

Ray Grigg has been a teacher of English literary history, fine arts, cultural history, and world religions in the British Columbia senior secondary school system for over twenty years. He holds two degrees from the University of British Columbia and has traveled extensively in over forty countries. He now lives with his wife on Quadra Island, British Columbia. He is a Taoist Scholar and author of the best-selling classics, *The Tao of Relationships* and *The Tao of Being: A Think and Do Workbook.*

Books about Taoism and Related Matters

Brand, Stuart, ed. **The Next Whole Earth Catalog**. New York: Point Random House, 1980.

Bynner, Witter. **The Way of Life According to Laotzu**. New York: Capricorn Books, 1962.

Capra, Fritjof. **The Tao of Physics**. Berkeley, CA: Shambala, 1975.

Feng, Gai-fu, and Jane English. **Tao Te Ching**. New York: Alfred A. Knopf, 1972.

Grigg, Ray. **The Tao of Being: A Think and Do Workbook**. Atlanta, GA: Humanics New Age, 1989.

Grigg, Ray. **The Tao of Relationships**. Atlanta, GA: Humanics New Age, 1988.

Heider, John. **The Tao of Leadership**. Atlanta, GA: Humanics New Age, 1985.

Medhurst, Spurgeon. **The Tao-Teh-King**. Wheaton, IL: The Theosophical Publishing House, 1972.

Messing, Robert. **The Tao of Management**. Atlanta, GA: Humanics New Age, 1989.

Schmidt, K.O. **Tao Te Ching (Lao Tzu's Book of Life)**. Lakemont, GA: CSA Press, 1975.

Schwenk, Theodore. **Sensitive Chaos**. New York: Schocken Books, 1965. Vanden Broek, Goldian, ed. **Less Is More: the Art of Voluntary Poverty**. Harper Colophon Books. New York: Harper & Row, 1978.

Waley, Arthur. **The Way and Its Power**. New York: Grove Press, 1958.

Watts, Alan, and Al Chung-liang Huang. **Tao the Watercourse Way**. New York: Pantheon Books, 1975.

Wilhelm, Richard, and Cary Baynes, trans. **I Ching, or the Book of Changes**. Princeton, NJ: Princeton University Press, 1967.

Wing, R.L. **The Tao of Power: Lao Tzu's Classic Guide to Leadership, Influence, and Excellence**. Garden City, NY: Doubleday & Company, Inc., 1986.